BASIC BIOGRAPHIES

Helen Keller

by Cynthia Amoroso and Robert B. Noyed

What if you could not see, speak, or hear? That is how a woman named Helen Keller lived.

Helen Keller could not see, speak, or hear.

Helen was born in Alabama on June 27, 1880. When she was just one year old, she became very ill. She almost died.

Helen was born in this house in 1880.

Helen got better. But she could no longer see or hear. She did not learn to speak as a young child.

This is Helen at age seven.

Life was hard for Helen and her family. Helen did not know what her family was saying or doing. She could not tell people what she needed.

Helen could not talk to her family.

Helen's parents found a teacher to help her. The teacher's name was Annie Sullivan. Annie came to live with Helen's family.

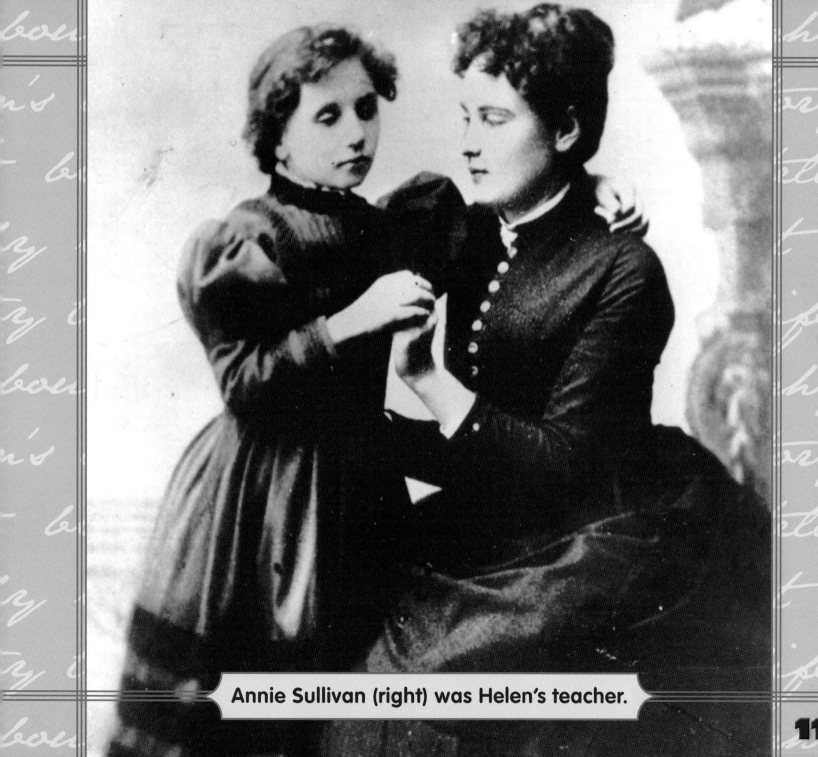

Annie Sullivan (right) was Helen's teacher.

Annie taught Helen using touch. She spelled words on Helen's hands.

The first word Helen learned was *water*. Helen learned very quickly.

Annie spelled words on Helen's hand.

Annie helped Helen learn to speak and to write. Helen learned to read **braille** with her fingertips. Annie even went with Helen to **college**.

Helen finished college in 1904.

People all over the world wanted to learn about Helen. She gave speeches and wrote books. She met many **famous** people.

Helen (center) met U.S. President Eisenhower in 1953.

Helen and Annie were together until Annie died in 1936. Then a woman named Polly Thomson helped Helen.

Helen and Polly (right) met Eleanor Roosevelt (left).

Helen died on June 1, 1968. She could not see or hear, but she did not let that stop her from being an important person.

Helen lived to be almost 88 years old.

Glossary

braille (BRAYL): Braille is a type of writing with an alphabet of raised dots that people read with their fingertips. Helen read books written in Braille.

college (KOL-ij): College is a school people go to after high school. Helen went to college.

famous (FAY-muss): A person who is famous is known by lots of people. Helen became famous.

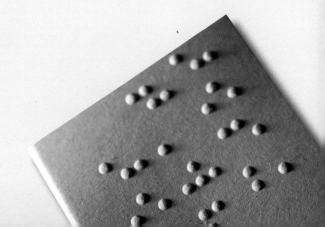

To Find Out More

Books

Adler, David A., and John C. Wallner. *Helen Keller.* New York: Holiday House, 2006.

Cline-Ransom, Lesa. *Helen Keller: The World In Her Heart.* New York: Collins, 2008.

Dolan, Sean. *Helen Keller.* Danbury, CT: Children's Press, 2006.

Web Sites

Visit our Web site for links about Helen Keller:
childsworld.com/links

Note to Parents, Teachers, and Librarians: We routinely verify our Web links to make sure they are safe and active sites. So encourage your readers to check them out!

Index

About the Authors

Cynthia Amoroso has worked as an elementary school teacher and a high school English teacher. Writing children's books is another way for her to share her passion for the written word.

Robert B. Noyed has worked as a newspaper reporter and in the communications department for a Minnesota school district. He enjoys the challenge and accomplishment of writing children's books.

On the cover: Helen Keller (left) touches her teacher's face.

Published by The Child's World®
1980 Lookout Drive • Mankato, MN 56003-1705
800-599-READ • www.childsworld.com

ACKNOWLEDGMENTS
The Child's World®: Mary Berendes, Publishing Director
The Design Lab: Design and production
Red Line Editorial: Editorial direction

PHOTO CREDITS: AP Images, cover, 5, 7, 11, 13, 15, 19, 21; Fabio Bustamante/iStockphoto, cover, 1, 14, 22; Gerhard Sisters/Library of Congress, 3; Walter Sanders/Getty Images, 9; Charles P. Gorry/AP Images, 17

Printed in the United States of America in Mankato, Minnesota.
June 2011
PA02099

LIBRARY OF CONGRESS CATALOGING-IN-PUBLICATION DATA
Amoroso, Cynthia.
 Helen Keller / by Cynthia Amoroso and Robert B. Noyed.
  p. cm. — (Basic biographies)
 Includes index.
 ISBN 978-1-60253-341-7 (library bound : alk. paper)
 1. Keller, Helen, 1880-1968—Juvenile literature. 2. Deafblind women--United States—Biography—Juvenile literature. 3. Deafblind people—United States—Biography—Juvenile literature. 4. Sullivan, Annie, 1866-1936—Juvenile literature. I. Noyed, Robert B. II. Title. III. Series.
 HV1624.K4A49 2010
 362.4'1092—dc22 [B]   2009029369